Introduction

Daniel is a favorite Bible character of most children. Even preschoolers know about Daniel's night in the lions' den. Young and old alike are inspired by the decision of Daniel and his three friends not to compromise their stand for God by eating King Nebuchadnezzar's food and drinking his wine. God's response to both these steps of faith was protection and blessing.

The stories and activities in this book cover the main events of Daniel's life as found in the book of Daniel. Students will enjoy learning about him through puzzles, crafts, action rhymes and songs, word games, and many other fun, creative activities. Most activities require that students use their Bibles to find or check their answers. (**Note:** This book uses the *New International Version* for scripture references.) A complete answer key is provided on pages 47 and 48 for your convenience.

The book is divided into five stories of Daniel with related activities: Daniel and His Friends, Daniel Explains the King's Dream, Daniel Explains Another Dream, Strange Writing on the Wall, and A Night with Lions. Students will discover for themselves the importance of faith in God as they see how Daniel stayed true while living as a captive in an idol-worshiping land among ungodly people. He not only managed to remain faithful to God, but he also prospered in the work the king gave him to do.

Some of the stories in the book of Daniel have been omitted either because Daniel is not involved, as in the story of the fiery furnace, or because the content of the story is on an adult level and not easily understood by children, such as Daniel's dreams and visions of the future.

A bulletin board is provided on pages 4 and 5 that can be used throughout the study of Daniel. Some of the activity pages are about Daniel, while others are application activities to help students look at their own relationship with God and other people. It also helps them discover what God wants them to do. The stories of Daniel's life were included in the Bible not just to inform us about one of God's great men, but to help us learn important truths about living for the Lord in a world that doesn't love Him. Make sure your students understand how each story applies to their own personal lives.

"Daniel" Bulletin Board

Directions

1. Cover a bulletin board with white paper.
2. Print the explanation of Daniel's life on a long strip of yellow or gold paper and mount it across the bottom of the board.
3. Use yellow ribbon or yarn to divide the rest of the board into six equal parts.
4. Color and cut out the figure of Daniel below. Mount it at the center of the board as shown. Cut Daniel's name from black paper and mount it above the figure of Daniel.
5. Before or after each lesson on Daniel, cut out the appropriate sentence strip from page 5 and mount it as shown above. Let students draw pictures to illustrate the story and add them above the sentence strip.

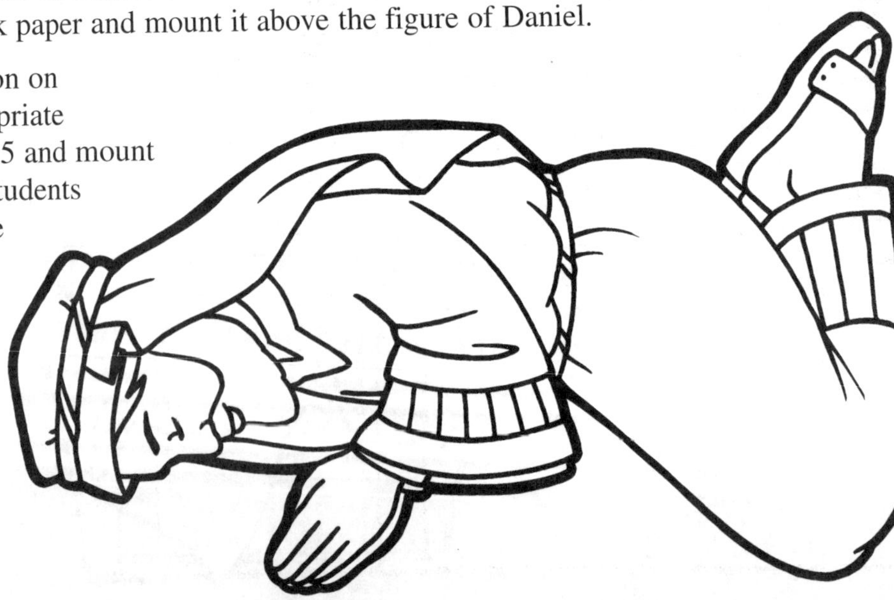

Editorial Project Manager
Lorin E. Klistoff, M. A.

Managing Editor
Karen J. Goldfluss, M.S. Ed.

Illustrator
Renée Christine Yates

Cover Artist
Brenda DiAntonis

Art Manager
Kevin Barnes

Imaging
James Edward Grace
Craig Gunnell

Publisher
Mary D. Smith, M.S. Ed.

Bible Stories & Activities

Daniel

Author

Mary Tucker

Teacher Created Resources, Inc.
6421 Industry Way
Westminster, CA 92683
www.teachercreated.com
ISBN-1-4206-7055-7

©2006 *Teacher Created Resources, Inc.*
Made in U.S.A.

The classroom teacher may reproduce copies of materials in this book for classroom use only. The reproduction of any part for an entire school or school system is strictly prohibited. No part of this publication may be transmitted, stored, or recorded in any form without written permission from the publisher.

Table of Contents

©Teacher Created Resources, Inc.

Bulletin Board Strips

He made wise choices about food and drink.

God helped him explain the king's dream.

He explained another dream and gave the king advice.

He read and explained God's writing on the wall.

He survived a night with hungry lions.

Daniel and His Friends

(Based on Daniel 1)

King Nebuchadnezzar and his Babylonian army had attacked Jerusalem and taken many of its people as captives back to Babylon. The king decided he wanted to train some of the best young Jewish men to serve in his palace. He ordered his chief official to choose the men and oversee their training in Babylonian writing and literature. They were to eat food from the king's table and be trained for three years to make them ready to enter the king's service.

Among the young men chosen were four friends: Daniel, Hananiah, Mishael, and Azariah. The first thing the chief official did was give them Babylonian names. Daniel became Belteshazzar, Hananiah became Shadrach, Mishael became Meshach, and Azariah became Abednego. Far from home, among ungodly people, the four young men began their training.

When Daniel and his friends were served rich food and wine from the king's table, he immediately decided to ask for something different. He and his friends wanted to honor God, even though they were living among people who did not worship Him. The problem was that the Babylonians worshiped idols and they always offered the first part of their food to their idols. Besides that, God had given the Jews specific rules about what kinds of food to eat and which ones to avoid. What could Daniel and his three friends do? Daniel asked Nebuchadnezzar's chief official for permission to eat only vegetables and drink only water. God caused the man to respond kindly to Daniel, but he was afraid if he allowed them to eat what they wanted, their health would suffer. If they looked less healthy than the other Jewish men being trained for the king's service, the chief official might get into trouble. "He would have my head because of you," he told Daniel.

Daniel talked their guard into allowing them to eat vegetables and drink water for 10 days. If, after that amount of time, the four of them still looked as healthy as the others, then they could continue eating their special diet and no one would have any reason to complain about it. Their guard agreed to the 10-day test. After 10 days Daniel and his three friends looked healthier and better nourished than all the other men being trained. They were allowed to keep eating vegetables and drinking water in place of the king's food and wine.

God blessed Daniel and his friends for honoring Him. At the end of the training period, the king talked with all those who had been trained and he found that Daniel, Shadrach, Meshach, and Abednego knew more than all the others. They were 10 times better than even his magicians and enchanters in every area of wisdom and understanding!

Gifts from God

Directions: All the other Jewish men went along with what the ungodly king wanted, but Daniel and his friends honored God. What did God do for them for honoring Him? Decode the words to complete the verse that tells what God gave them. Look up Daniel 1:17 to check your work.

A	B	C	D	E	F	G	H	I	J	K	L	M
➴	✳	✤	✦	✧	★	✪	☞	✱	✹	✢	✝	↔
N	**O**	**P**	**Q**	**R**	**S**	**T**	**U**	**V**	**W**	**X**	**Y**	**Z**
❺	✡	✏	❤	❢	)	↕	♠	➢	⚯	✗	✚	✌

TO THESE FOUR YOUNG MEN GOD GAVE

___ ___ ___ ___ ___ ___ ___ ___ ___ **AND**
✢ ❺ ✡ ⚯ ✝ ✧ ✦ ✪ ✧

___ ___ ___ ___ ___ ___ ___ ___ ___ ___ ___ ___ ___ **OF**
♠ ❺ ✦ ✧ ❢) ↕ ➴ ❺ ✦ ✱ ❺ ✪

ALL KINDS OF ___ ___ ___ ___ ___ ___ ___ ___ ___ ___ **AND**
✝ ✱ ↕ ✧ ❢ ➴ ↕ ♠ ❢ ✧

___ ___ ___ ___ ___ ___ ___ ___. **AND DANIEL COULD**
✝ ✧ ➴ ❢ ❺ ✱ ❺ ✪

UNDERSTAND ___ ___ ___ ___ ___ ___ ___ **AND**
➢ ✱) ✱ ✡ ❺)

___ ___ ___ ___ ___ ___ **OF ALL KINDS.**
✦ ❢ ✧ ➴ ↔)

"True to God" Action Rhyme

Directions: Divide students into two groups. Have group one read and act out the part of the king's official and guard. Have group two read and act out the part of Daniel and his friends.

King's Official	
We've brought you all here to learn how to serve,	*(Sweep arm toward other group.)*
To test your intelligence, wisdom, and nerve.	*(Pat head with one finger.)*
Daniel and His Friends	
Uh-oh, what now? What should we do?	*(Shrug shoulders and look at each other.)*
Help us, oh God, to stay true to You.	*(Pray.)*
King's Official	
We'll serve you fine food from the king's own table.	*(Lick lips and rub stomach.)*
And you can drink as much wine as you are able.	*(Pretend to drink.)*
Daniel and His Friends	
No thanks. We want to stay true to our God.	*(Shake head "no"; hold hand out to say "stop.")*
Could we eat something else, even if it is odd?	*(Fold hands as if asking a favor.)*
King's Official	
I'm sorry, but if you aren't properly fed	*(Shake head "no" and look scared.)*
And you get sick, it could mean my head!	*(Swipe finger across neck.)*
Daniel and His Friends	
We'll ask the guard for a 10-day test	*(Hold up all fingers on both hands.)*
Of veggies and water. We'll beat all the rest!	*(Point to other group.)*
King's Guard	
For 10 days I've fed you what you asked me to.	*(Hold up all fingers on both hands.)*
Now you look better than all of them do!	*(Point over shoulder.)*
Daniel and His Friends	
We're so healthy and wise; the king is impressed!	*(Hold up both hands in victory.)*
Because we were true to our God, we've been blessed.	*(Cross hands over heart.)*

©Teacher Created Resources, Inc.

Bible Story Acrostic

Directions: Use the clues from the story in Daniel 1 to fill in the words of the acrostic. Look up the Bible verses if you need help.

11. ___ ___ **N** ___ ’ ___

2. ___ **E** ___ ___ ___ ___ ___ ___ ___

1. **B** ___ ___ ___ ___ ___ ___

4. ___ ___ **U** ___ ___

3. **C** ___ ___ ___ ___ OF COURT OFFICIALS

5. **H** ___ ___ ___ ___ ___ ___ ___

7. ___ **A** ___ ___ ___ ___ ___ ___

8. **D** ___ ___ ___ ___ ___

12. ___ ___ **N** ___

6. ___ **E** ___ ___ INFORMED

Z

9. ___ **Z** ___ ___ ___ ___ ___

10. ___ ___ ___ ___ **A** ___ ___

13. ___ ___ **R** ___ ___ ___ ___ ___ ___ ___

1. Nebuchadnezzar was from this place. (Daniel 1:1)
2. He besieged and conquered this town. (Daniel 1:1)
3. Nebuchadnezzar told him to train Israelite men to serve in the palace. (Daniel 1:3–4)

4.–5.–6. The kind of men to be chosen (Daniel 1:4)

7.–8.–9.–10. Four of the young men to be trained (Daniel 1:6)

11. The men being trained were given rich food from the _____ table. (Daniel 1:5)
12. They were given this to drink. (Daniel 1:5)
13. The length of the training time (Daniel 1:5)

Stand Up for the Lord Song

Directions: Sing the song and do the actions. Then, answer the questions.

(**Tune:** "If You're Happy and You Know It")

Stand up for the Lord and do what's right.

(Stand tall with hand on heart.)

Speak right up and be a shining light.

("Twinkle" fingers like stars.)

Like Daniel long ago,

(Motion with thumb over shoulder.)

When things are wrong, say "No!"

(Hit palm of hand with fist.)

Just stand up for the Lord and do what's right.

(Stand tall, stretch arms up, and clap hands twice overhead.)

Questions

When is it hard to stand up for the Lord and do what is right? ______________________

____

Read Daniel's story in Daniel 1. Why did it take courage to do what he did? ____________

____

How can you find the courage to stand up for the Lord even if no one else is? ____________

____

©Teacher Created Resources, Inc.

Faithfulness Mobile

Make this mobile and hang it in your room as a reminder to be faithful to God every day as Daniel was.

Materials

- patterns (pages 11 and 12)
- poster board
- 2 plastic drinking straws
- crayons or colored markers
- scissors
- hole punch
- string or thread
- stapler and staples

Finished Product

Directions

1. Copy the patterns onto poster board and color them.
2. Read the words on each pattern. Discuss them together.
3. Cut out each pattern and punch a hole in the top.
4. Staple the two straws together in the middle, forming an X.
5. Hang the heart from the center of the straw X with a 10" length of string or thread.
6. Hang each of the other patterns from an end of the straw X with a 6" length of string or thread.
7. Tie a length of string or thread to the center of the straw X to hang the mobile.

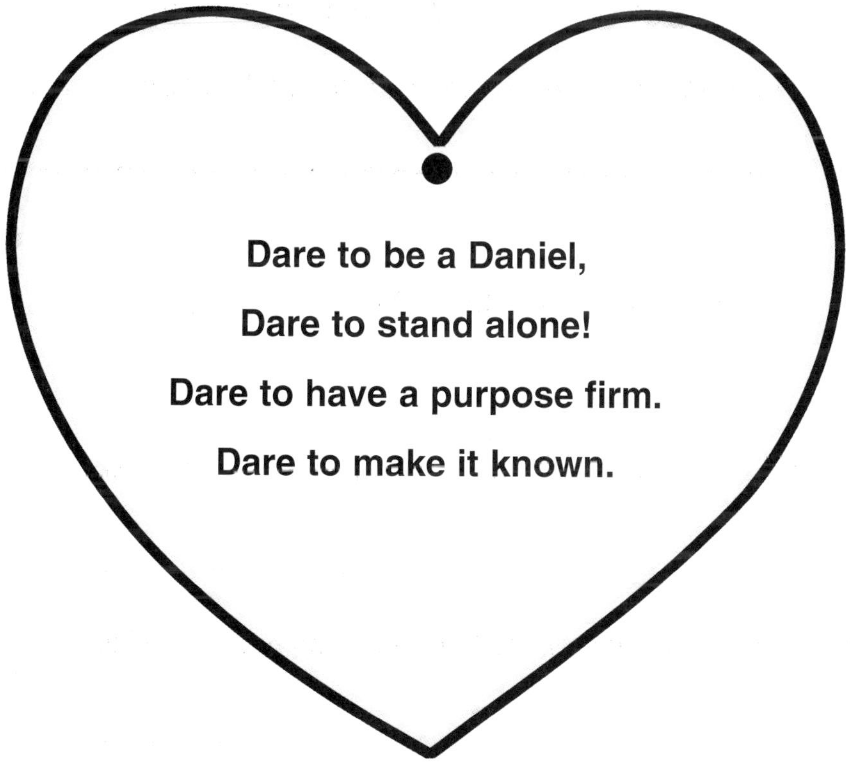

Faithfulness Mobile

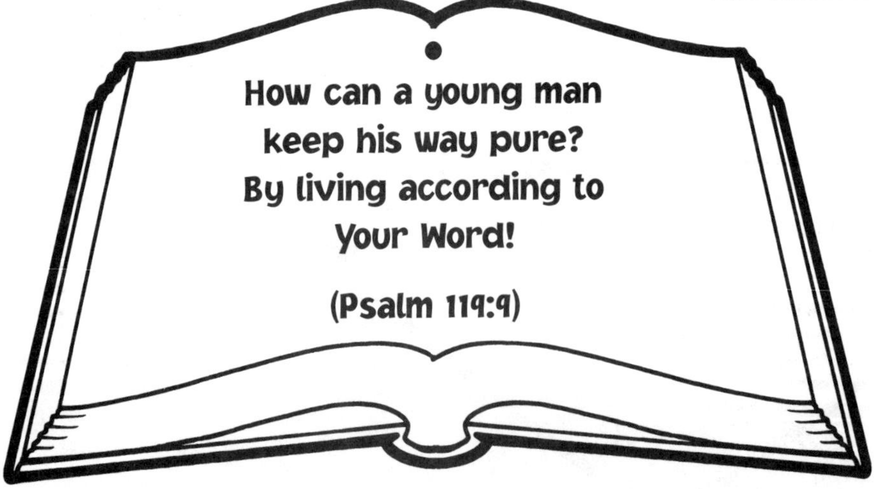

Daniel's Choice

Directions: Look at the food pictured below. Daniel knew God did not want him and his friends to eat the food from the king's table because it had been offered to idols. Circle the foods Daniel chose and cross out the ones he and his friends refused to eat. If you need help, look up Daniel 1:12. Then, <u>in the empty box</u> draw what Daniel and his friends chose to drink instead of the king's wine.

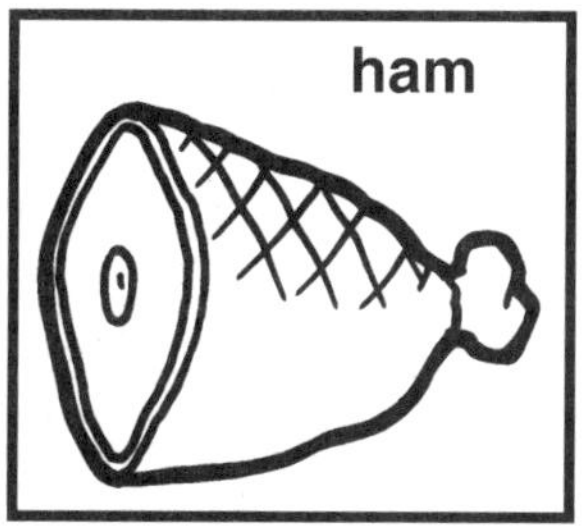

©Teacher Created Resources, Inc.

Daniel Explains the King's Dream

(Based on Daniel 2)

King Nebuchadnezzar was troubled. He was worried about the strange dream he had been having. He summoned his magicians, astrologers, and wise men to explain the dream for him. They told the king, "Tell us the dream and we will explain it."

But Nebuchadnezzar didn't want to tell them the dream. If he did, then they could just make up an explanation for it. How would he know it wasn't the truth? If they told him what he had dreamed, then explained it, then he would believe them.

"There is not a man on earth who can do that!" the astrologers replied. "No king has ever asked such an impossible thing of any magician or astrologer. What you ask is too difficult." Their attitude made the king so furious, he ordered all the wise men in Babylon executed.

When the king's order was issued, all the wise men were rounded up to be executed. Even Daniel and his three friends were brought in, since they also were considered wise men. Daniel asked the commander of the king's guard, "Why did the king issue such a harsh order?" The commander explained what had happened. Daniel immediately went to talk to Nebuchadnezzar and asked him for time so he could explain the king's dream. Nebuchadnezzar was so glad at the possibility of having his dream explained, he postponed the executions.

Daniel went home and asked his three friends, Shadrach, Meshach, and Abednego, to pray for him and to ask God to reveal the king's dream to him. During the night the mystery was revealed to Daniel in a vision. Daniel praised God for helping him. "Praise be to the name of God for ever and ever; wisdom and power are his. He reveals deep and hidden things." (Daniel 2:20, 22a)

Daniel went again to speak to the commander of the king's guard. "Do not execute the wise men," he said. "Take me to the king and I will explain his dream." The commander took him to the king at once. When the king asked him if he could really explain the dream, Daniel said, "There is a God in heaven who reveals mysteries. He has shown King Nebuchadnezzar what will happen in days to come. This mystery has been revealed to me, not because I have greater wisdom than other living men, but so you may know the interpretation." Then, he told the king exactly what he had dreamed.

The king had dreamed of a large statue with a gold head, silver chest and arms, bronze thighs and stomach, and iron and clay legs and feet. A rock struck the statue and smashed the feet. The whole statue was broken to pieces. The wind blew all the pieces away, but the rock became a huge mountain. The statue, Daniel explained, represented the kingdoms that would come after Nebuchadnezzar's. Some would be weaker than his; others would be stronger. The rock stood for the kingdom God would set up that would never be destroyed.

King Nebuchadnezzer bowed before Daniel and honored him for his wisdom. He promoted him to a high position in the government and gave him many gifts. Daniel ruled over the whole province of Babylon and was in charge of all the wise men. His three friends, Shadrach, Meshach, and Abednego, became his administrators.

Nebuchadnezzar said that Daniel's God was the God of gods, but he did not worship Him. Daniel gave credit to God for explaining the dream and God blessed him for his faithfulness.

Mysteries Revealed

Directions: Daniel praised God for revealing the mystery of King Nebuchadnezzar's dream. Decode the words below to complete what Daniel said about God. Look up Daniel 2:21–22 to check your work.

A	B	C	D	E	F	G	H	I	J	K	L	M
6	5	4	3	2	1	0	9	8	7	10	11	12

N	O	P	Q	R	S	T	U	V	W	X	Y	Z
20	19	18	17	16	15	14	13	26	25	24	23	22

HE CHANGES ___ ___ ___ ___ ___ AND
14 8 12 2 15

___ ___ ___ ___ ___ ___ ___;
15 2 6 15 19 20 15

HE SETS UP ___ ___ ___ ___ ___ AND DEPOSES THEM.
10 8 20 0 15

HE GIVES ___ ___ ___ ___ ___ ___ TO THE WISE AND
25 8 15 3 19 12

___ ___ ___ ___ ___ ___ ___ ___ ___ TO THE DISCERNING . . . .
10 20 19 25 11 2 3 0 2

HE KNOWS WHAT LIES IN ___ ___ ___ ___ ___ ___ ___ ___,
3 6 16 10 20 2 15 15

AND ___ ___ ___ ___ ___ DWELLS WITH HIM. (Daniel 2:21–22)
11 8 0 9 14

"A Dream Explained" Rap

Directions: Say the rap together, snapping your fingers or clapping your hands to set the rhythm.

King Nebuchadnezzar, he had a dream
That worried him so he wanted to scream!
He called his magicians and every wise man,
And said, "Explain my dream if you can."
"Of course," they said. (How easy it seemed.)
"Go ahead and tell us what you dreamed."
But the king refused, so what could they do?
How could they explain what no one knew?
When Daniel heard about the dream, he prayed
And asked the Lord to come to his aid.
His friends prayed too, and in a vision one night
The dream was revealed and Daniel saw the light.
He went to the king and said, "Listen to me;
There's a God who reveals all mysteries.
In your dream He was showing you
What will happen in the future, and it's all true."
Then Daniel explained, bit by bit,
The dream of the king, every part of it.
King Nebuchadnezzar bowed down low
Before the wisest man he ever could know.
He promoted Daniel, and when he was done,
Daniel ruled over all Babylon.
Daniel gave credit to God for it all
Because God had answered when Daniel called.

 ©Teacher Created Resources, Inc.

Who Did What?

Directions: To match the people with what they did, write the correct letters next to each person or group of people. If you need help, read the story in Daniel 2.

______________________ **1.** King Nebuchadnezzar

______________________ **2.** The king's magicians and wise men

______________________ **3.** Daniel

______________________ **4.** Daniel's friends: Hananiah, Mishael, and Azariah

A. Explained the king's dream

B. Threatened to kill all the magicians and wise men in the land

C. Bowed before Daniel

D. Prayed that God would reveal the king's dream

E. Told the king no one could explain the dream if God did not reveal it

F. Gave God credit for revealing the dream's explanation

G. Had a strange dream

H. Was promoted to ruler over all Babylon

I. Worshiped God

J. Said Daniel's God was the God of gods, but did not worship Him

K. Were rounded up by the king's officers to be executed

Joseph and Daniel

Directions: Another Bible person who was able to explain dreams was Joseph. Compare Joseph's experience with Daniel's. Complete the stories by filling in the missing words. Then find the words in the puzzle and circle them.

K	Z	R	M	Y	S	T	E	R	Y	L	T	E	L	L
N	D	R	E	A	M	R	Q	C	U	G	G	L	D	C
O	D	D	H	V	O	Z	A	W	B	L	T	Y	Z	A
W	W	G	V	N	E	J	V	N	D	R	E	A	M	N
N	I	J	O	Q	T	A	Z	F	S	N	N	R	B	N
H	S	H	B	D	V	W	L	P	R	W	Q	L	Q	O
K	E	S	U	B	M	I	T	S	Z	L	E	M	N	T
M	R	E	X	P	L	A	I	N	C	H	A	R	G	E

JOSEPH

Pharaoh said to Joseph, "I had a ____________________, and no one can interpret it. But I have heard it said of you that when you hear a ____________________ you can interpret it."

"I ____________________ do it," Joseph replied to Pharaoh, "but ______________ will give Pharaoh the ____________________ he desires."

Then Pharaoh said to Joseph, "Since God has made all of this ____________________ to you, there is no one so discerning and ____________________ as you. You shall be in ____________________ of my palace, and all my people are to ____________________ to your orders." (Genesis 41:15–16, 39–40a)

DANIEL

The king asked Daniel, "Are you able to ____________________ me what I saw in my dream and interpret it?"

Daniel replied, "No wise man, enchanter, magician, or diviner can ____________________ to the king the ____________________ he has asked about, but there is a God in heaven who ____________________ mysteries."

Then King Nebuchadnezzar fell prostrate before Daniel and paid him ____________________. Then the king placed Daniel in a ______________ position and lavished many gifts on him. He made him ____________________ over the entire province of Babylon and placed him in charge of all its wise men. (Daniel 2:26–28a, 46a, 48)

 ©Teacher Created Resources, Inc.

What Happened When?

Directions: Look at the pictures carefully. In the boxes, number the pictures from 1 to 6 to show the order in which they happened. If you need help, read the complete story in Daniel 2.

"Praise God" Craft

Daniel praised God before and after He revealed the king's dream. God wants you to praise Him, too. What can you praise Him for? Cut apart the praise reminders on page 21. Put them in the praise pack after you make it. Keep it on the refrigerator door. Every time you open the refrigerator, take one of the reminders from the praise pack and read it. Then, take a minute to praise God as Daniel did. Invite your family to use the praise pack, too.

Materials

- small cardboard box (such as a flavored gelatin or pudding box)
- construction paper or paint and paintbrush
- crayons or colored markers
- magnetic tape or small magnets
- praise reminders on page 21
- scissors
- pattern below
- glue
- decorative stickers

Directions

1. Cut the lid off the box and throw it away.
2. Cover the whole box with construction paper (your choice of color) and glue it down, or paint the box your favorite color.
3. Color and cut out the pattern on this page. Glue it on the front of the box.
4. Glue magnetic tape or magnets on the back of the completed box.
5. Add decorative stickers.
6. Put the praise reminders, cut from page 21, in the pack and attach the pack to the refrigerator door.

Why praise God every day?

Because He loves it when you pray.

Tell Him thanks for who He is.

Let God know your heart is His.

Finished Product

Praise Reminders

See page 20 for directions.

PRAISE GOD

because He knows everything and can do anything!

"Praise be to the name of God for ever and ever; wisdom and power are his."

(Daniel 2:20)

PRAISE GOD

because He loves you.

"I have loved you with an everlasting love; I have drawn you with loving-kindness."

(Jeremiah 31:3)

PRAISE GOD

because He is with you.

"God has said, 'Never will I leave you; never will I forsake you.'"

(Hebrews 13:5)

PRAISE GOD

for the way He made you.

"For you created my inmost being; you knit me together in my mother's womb. I praise you because I am fearfully and wonderfully made."

(Psalm 139:13–14a)

PRAISE GOD

for sending His Son to earth to die for your sins.

"For God so loved the world that he gave his one and only Son, that whoever believes in him shall not perish but have eternal life."

(John 3:16)

PRAISE GOD

because He listens when you pray.

"Before they call I will answer; while they are still speaking I will hear."

(Isaiah 65:24)

PRAISE GOD

for His wonderful Word, the Bible!

"Your word is a lamp to my feet and a light for my path."

(Psalm 119:105)

PRAISE GOD

because He has a home for you in heaven.

"In my Father's house are many rooms; . . . I am going there to prepare a place for you."

(John 14:2)

PRAISE GOD

for taking care of you and providing for you.

"And my God will meet all your needs according to his glorious riches in Christ Jesus."

(Philippians 4:19)

Daniel Explains Another Dream

(Based on Daniel 4)

King Nebuchadnezzar had another strange dream. He called for his wise men and magicians and asked them to explain the dream. They could not. Then, the king remembered that Daniel had explained a dream for him once before, so he summoned Daniel.

Nebuchadnezzar told Daniel what he had dreamed. He said he had seen a large, strong tree. Its leaves were beautiful, and it had lots of fruit on it. Animals came to lie down in the shade of the tree, and many birds built nests in its branches. Then, the king saw a messenger come down from heaven. The messenger said, "Cut down the tree and trim its branches; strip off its leaves and scatter its fruit." Then, the messenger talked about the tree stump. He said, "Let him live with the animals among the plants of the earth. Let his mind be changed from that of a man, and let him be given the mind of an animal, till seven times pass by for him."

When Nebuchadnezzar finished telling Daniel about his dream, he noticed that Daniel was troubled. Daniel explained that the tree in the dream represented the king. Nebuchadnezzar was great and strong, but he was going to be cut down like the tree and driven away from people. For seven years he would live outside with the wild animals and would eat grass like a cow. Nebuchadnezzar would live like an animal until he was willing to honor God and admit that God was in control, not him.

"O king, be pleased to accept my advice," Daniel said. "Renounce your sins by doing what is right, and your wickedness by being kind to the oppressed. It may be that your prosperity will continue." But Nebuchadnezzar was a proud man, and he did not listen to Daniel's good advice.

A year later, the king was walking on the roof of his palace, looking out over the city. "Look at this great city I have built," he said. "I have great power and majesty!"

The words were barely out of his mouth when a voice spoke from heaven: "King Nebuchadnezzar, your royal authority has been taken from you. You will live with the wild animals until you acknowledge that the Most High is sovereign over the kingdoms of men." Immediately, the king's dream came true. He lost his mind and was driven away from people. He wandered in the fields, eating grass like an animal. His hair grew long and shaggy, and his fingernails grew long like a bird's claws.

Finally, one day Nebuchadnezzar looked up toward heaven and praised God. His sanity was immediately restored. Nebuchadnezzar was an even greater king after that than he had been before. He had learned his lesson. He honored God and admitted that God was in control, not him. It was a humbling experience for a great king.

A King's Story

Directions: King Nebuchadnezzar told everyone about his dream, Daniel's explanation of it, and how it came true. The experience taught Nebuchadnezzar a great lesson about pride. Use the clues to discover the words. Then use the words to complete what King Nebuchadnezzar said.

CLUES

1. countries—N ___ ___ ___ ___ ___ ___

2. royal land—K ___ ___ ___ ___ ___ ___

3. forever and ever—E ___ ___ ___ ___ ___ ___

4. amazing things—W ___ ___ ___ ___ ___ ___

5. earth—W ___ ___ ___ ___

6. a Bible word for *things shown by God*—S ___ ___ ___ ___

7. opposite of "duty or obligation"—P ___ ___ ___ ___ ___ ___ ___

KING NEBUCHADNEZZAR, TO THE PEOPLES, ___ ___ ___ ___ ___ ___ ___ (1)

AND MEN OF EVERY LANGUAGE, WHO LIVE IN ALL THE ___ ___ ___ ___ ___ (5): . . .

IT IS MY ___ ___ ___ ___ ___ ___ ___ ___ (7) TO TELL YOU ABOUT THE

MIRACULOUS SIGNS AND WONDERS THAT THE MOST HIGH GOD HAS PERFORMED

FOR ME. HOW GREAT ARE HIS ___ ___ ___ ___ ___ (6), HOW MIGHTY HIS

___ ___ ___ ___ ___ ___ ___ (4)! HIS ___ ___ ___ ___ ___ ___ ___ (2)

IS AN ___ ___ ___ ___ ___ ___ ___ (3) KINGDOM; HIS DOMINION ENDURES

FROM GENERATION TO GENERATION. (Daniel 4:1–3)

Daniel's Advice

Directions: When God gave Daniel the explanation of the king's dream, Daniel wanted to help the king. Follow the directions to discover the advice Daniel gave Nebuchadnezzar.

1. Mark out every word that begins with **L**.
2. Mark out every word that ends with **W**.
3. Mark out every word that rhymes with *day*.
4. Write the remaining words in order on the lines.

let	may	Renounce	your	way	love
sins	now	by	doing	say	saw
pay	what	is	delay	long	right
and	few	your	show	wickedness	by
being	stay	listen	kind	below	to
pray	the	later	they	oppressed	how

Daniel said to the king, "Be pleased to accept my advice:

________ ________ ________ ________

________ ________ ________ ________, ________

________ ________ ________ ________

________ ________ ________ ________."

(Daniel 4:27a)

 ©Teacher Created Resources, Inc.

Daniel Obeys

It must have been hard for Daniel to tell King Nebuchadnezzar what his dream of a tree meant. Daniel knew that the dream meant bad things were ahead for the king. Did Daniel consider telling him something good so the king wouldn't get angry? Did Daniel think about telling the king that he couldn't explain his dream? Did Daniel want to run away and not give the king bad news? Why did Daniel dare to tell the king what God told him?

Directions: Hundreds of years after Daniel lived, the apostle John wrote about why we should obey God. Decode the Bible verse to find out what he said. Do you think this is why Daniel obeyed God? Look up 1 John 5:3a to check your work.

A	➽
B	✣
C	✞
D	✿
E	✹
F	☛
G	☆
H	❤
I	✜
L	✪
M	➤
N	①
O	♠
R	✶
S	❃
T	✠
V	➢
Y	↕

__ __ __ __   __ __   __ __ __ __
✠ ❤ ✜ ❃   ✜ ❃   ✪ ♠ ➢ ✹

__ __ __   __ __ __: __ __
☛ ♠ ✶   ☆ ♠ ✿   ✠ ♠

__ __ __ __   __ __ __
♠ ✣ ✹ ↕   ❤ ✜ ❃

__ __ __ __ __ __ __ __.
✞ ♠ ➤ ➤ ➽ ① ✿ ❃

The Problem of Pride

Directions: Nebuchadnezzar had a problem with pride, and God chose an unusual way to teach him humility. The Bible warns us about the dangers of pride. Starting at the arrow, write on the lines below every third word in the box. When you get to the end of a line, go to the beginning of the next line and keep counting. You will discover what God had King Solomon write about pride. Look up Proverbs 16:18 to check your work.

TAKE	**STOP**	**PRIDE**	**EVEN**	**KNOW**	**GOES**
AFTER	**NOW**	**BEFORE**	**YES**	**SINCE**	**DESTRUCTION**
THE	**WISE**	**A**	**HIS**	**HER**	**HAUGHTY**
BRAVE	**FOOLISH**	**SPIRIT**	**TOLD**	**TEACH**	**BEFORE**
GOD	**HAVE**	**A**	**THAT**	**SO**	**FALL**

"______________ ______________ ______________

______________________________, ______

______________ ______________

______________ ______ ______________."

How do you think Solomon's words proved true in King Nebuchadnezzar's life? Do you think Daniel had a problem with pride? How can you tell?

____

____

Wooden Plaque

We all need reminders to be humble, not proud. Make this plaque to hang on the wall or stick on a refrigerator as a reminder.

Materials

- patterns on page 28
- cardstock
- string or magnetic tape
- scissors
- crayons or colored markers
- white and colored glue
- red felt or construction paper
- craft sticks (four per child)

Finished Product

Directions

1. Copy the large heart onto cardstock.
2. Color the large heart and cut it out.
3. Make a frame with four craft sticks and glue them together.
4. Cut out a red felt or construction paper square slightly larger than the frame opening.
5. Glue the large heart on the felt or paper square.
6. Glue the felt or construction paper square behind the frame so the heart is centered in the frame opening. Let the glue dry.
7. Copy the small hearts, color them, and cut them out.
8. Glue one of the small hearts to each corner of the frame.
9. Use colored glue to draw a design on the craft stick frame. Let the glue dry.
10. Cut out a cardstock square to back the frame.
11. Glue the square to the back of the frame.
12. Attach string or magnetic tape to the back of the frame to hang it.

Wooden Plaque

Plaque Patterns

God opposes the proud
but gives grace to the humble.
Humble yourselves
before the Lord.
(James 4:6b, 10a)

 ©Teacher Created Resources, Inc.

Pride Song

Directions: Sing this song with the class.

(**Tune**: "B-I-N-G-O")

The Bible says, "Do not be proud, but have humility."

P-R-O-U-D, P-R-O-U-D, P-R-O-U-D,

I won't be proud, not me!

The Bible says a haughty spirit causes us to fall.

P-R-O-U-D, P-R-O-U-D, P-R-O-U-D,

I won't be proud at all!

There's nothing I can brag about except God's love, you see.

P-R-O-U-D, P-R-O-U-D, P-R-O-U-D,
I won't be proud, not me!

Questions

What does it mean to be humble? ______________________________

____

Why is it easier to be proud than humble? ______________________________

____

How can we keep pride from filling our hearts? ______________________________

____

©Teacher Created Resources, Inc.

Strange Writing on the Wall

(Based on Daniel 5)

King Belshazzar gave a great banquet for 1,000 of his nobles. He served delicious food and lots of alcoholic drinks. The king sat down to drink with his guests and must have drunk too much because he did a very foolish thing. He ordered the special gold and silver cups brought to him from the temple so he and his guests could drink out of them. King Nebuchadnezzar had stolen the cups from the Jewish temple at Jerusalem years before when he attacked and conquered the city. He took the cups and many Jewish captives back to Babylon with him. Apparently, the cups had been stored away somewhere and not used. Belshazzar decided it would show how powerful he was if he drank from the cups dedicated to the God of the Jews.

The cups were brought to the king and filled with wine. He and some other wicked people began drinking from them. As they drank, they praised their false gods and idols. In fact, they apparently praised every god except the true God to whom the cups had been dedicated. But God saw what was going on, and He had a lesson to teach Belshazzar. Suddenly, the fingers of a human hand appeared out of nowhere, writing a message on the plaster wall. The king watched in horror as the hand moved from letter to letter. He was so frightened, his face turned pale and his knees shook so he could not stand up.

Belshazzar called for his wise men to read the message and explain it to him. He promised to reward the person who could read the message with royal clothing and jewelry and make him the third highest ruler in the land. All the wise men came, but none of them could read or explain the message. Everyone was baffled. What could it mean? Suddenly, the party fun was over, and everyone was very serious.

The queen came into the banquet hall and told the king how Daniel had explained King Nebuchadnezzar's dreams years before. Daniel was the man to call to explain this mystery, so he was brought before Belshazzar. "I have heard that the spirit of the gods is in you and that you have insight, intelligence, and outstanding wisdom," the king said to him. He explained to Daniel what a great reward he would be given if he could read the message on the wall and explain it.

Daniel reminded Belshazzar what had happened to King Nebuchadnezzar who had been brought low by God because of his pride. Nebuchadnezzar had lived like an animal for seven years until he humbled himself and praised God. "But you his son," Daniel said, "have not humbled yourself, though you knew all this. Instead, you have set yourself up against the Lord of heaven. You did not honor the God who holds in his hand your life and all your ways." Daniel was not shy about telling the king how foolish and sinful he had been. Then Daniel read the message on the wall: MENE, MENE, TEKEL, PARSIN. He explained that it meant that God was going to bring Belshazzar's rule to an end because he did not measure up to what God wanted him to be. His kingdom would be divided between the Medes and the Persians.

Belshazzar rewarded Daniel as he had promised, but that very night the king was killed and Darius the Mede took over his kingdom. God's punishment of the foolish king was swift. It happened exactly as Daniel said it would. The proud king discovered that God was truly the One in control.

Daniel's Message

Directions: Complete what Daniel said to King Belshazzar. Fit the words into the crossword puzzle. **A** words go across; **D** words go down. Look up the Bible verses if you need help.

CLUES

Daniel agreed to explain the writing on the wall, but he told King Belshazzar he could keep his gifts and give the 8-D to someone else. (Daniel 5:17)

He pointed out that the king had not 1-A himself, though he knew what had happened to King Nebuchadnezzar because of his pride. (Daniel 5:22)

Belshazzar had set himself up against the Lord by drinking wine from the temple cups and he had 9-A false gods that could not 11-A or 5-A or 7-A. He did not 5-D the God who held his 2-D in his 6-D. (Daniel 5:23)

The writing on the wall said that Belshazzar had been weighed by God and found 4-A. His 3-D would soon 10-D. (Daniel 5:26–28)

God's Inscription

Directions: Daniel told Belshazzar that God sent the hand that wrote the inscription on the wall. Solve the clues. Then use the words to complete the meaning of God's inscription. Some clues have the first letter to help you. Look up Daniel 5:25–28 to check your work.

CLUES

1. Lord ___ ___ ___

2. Split or separated d ___ ___ ___ ___ ___ ___

3. Weight measured w ___ ___ ___ ___ ___ ___

4. Opposite of nights ___ ___ ___ ___

5. Opposite of beginning ___ ___ ___

6. Machines that weigh objects s ___ ___ ___ ___ ___

7. Opposite of "me" ___ ___ ___

8. The land over which a king rules k ___ ___ ___ ___ ___ ___

MENE, MENE, TEKEL, PARSIN

MENE: ___ ___ ___ has numbered the ___ ___ ___ ___ of your reign
1 4

and brought it to an ___ ___ ___.
5

TEKEL: ___ ___ ___ have been ___ ___ ___ ___ ___ ___ ___ on the
7 3

___ ___ ___ ___ ___ ___ and found wanting.
6

PERES: Your ___ ___ ___ ___ ___ ___ ___ is
8

___ ___ ___ ___ ___ ___ ___ and given to the Medes and Persians.
2

 ©Teacher Created Resources, Inc.

Palace Maze

Directions: Help Daniel find his way through the maze to the palace to explain the writing on the wall to King Belshazzar.

In What Order?

Directions: Look at the pictures carefully. Number them from 1 to 6 to show the order in which they happened. If you need help, read the complete story in Daniel 5.

 ©Teacher Created Resources, Inc.

Action Song

Directions: Sing this song with your students.

(**Tune:** "The Farmer in the Dell")

The writing on the wall, the writing on the wall,

(*Raise hand in air and pretend to write.*)

God sent a message in the writing on the wall.

(*Point to heaven; then continue writing.*)

The king was very scared, the king was very scared.

(*Look very scared.*)

He shook so hard he couldn't stand. The king was very scared.

(*Shake and knock knees together.*)

Daniel was called in, Daniel was called in.

(*Motion with arm as if for someone to join you.*)

No one could figure out the words till Daniel was called in.

(*Scratch head in bewilderment.*)

Daniel told the king, Daniel told the king,

(*Fold arms across chest and look serious.*)

"You didn't honor God and now your kingdom soon will end."

(*Wag index finger as if scolding someone.*)

We all should honor God, we all should honor God.

(*Raise hands over head and look toward heaven.*)

Those who don't risk punishment. We all should honor God.

(*Kneel down, look down, then raise hands to God again.*)

©Teacher Created Resources, Inc.

What They Got

Directions: King Belshazzar and Daniel both got something the night a hand wrote on the king's wall. Match each man with what he received by writing the correct letters on the lines next to him. Look up Daniel 5:25–30 to check your answers.

DANIEL

____, ____, ____

BELSHAZZAR

____, ____, ____

A. gold chain

B. lost his kingdom

C. death

D. important job

E. purple clothing

F. a message from God

©Teacher Created Resources, Inc.

The Writing Hand

Directions

1. Color and cut out the picture and the hand on this page.
2. Glue the hand to a craft stick.
3. Cut a slit in the picture along the line.
4. Stick the hand through the slit at the back and move it across the picture.
5. Read the story of the writing hand in Daniel 5.

A Night with Lions

(Based on Daniel 6)

King Darius appointed 120 men to help rule his kingdom. He called them *satraps*. He appointed three men to be over the satraps as administrators. One of the administrators was Daniel. The satraps had to report to the administrators so the king did not have to be concerned with them. Daniel did such a good job, King Darius decided to promote him to rule over the whole kingdom. This made the satraps and other administrators jealous. They looked for some wrongdoing in Daniel's life so they could report him to the king and cause trouble for him. But Daniel was a godly man, and his enemies could not find even one thing he was doing wrong! He was completely trustworthy. "We will never find any charges against this man Daniel," his enemies said, "unless it has something to do with the law of his God."

That is when the administrators and satraps came up with a wicked plan to get rid of Daniel. Some of them went to the king and began flattering him. They convinced him that he was so great, no one should pray to anyone but him! King Darius ate it up and fell into their trap. They convinced him to write a decree that no person was allowed to pray to any god or man except Darius for 30 days. Anyone who disobeyed the king's decree would be thrown into a den of lions!

Darius had the decree put into writing and everyone began obeying it, everyone that is except Daniel. It would take more than a decree from the king to make Daniel be unfaithful to God. It was his habit to pray to God three times a day, and he went right on doing it in spite of the king's decree. Daniel did not hide in a corner of his house to pray where no one would see him. He kneeled down next to the open windows in his home where everyone could see him pray.

Of course, this made Daniel's enemies happy. They finally could report him for doing something wrong! They went as a group to tell King Darius, "You issued a decree that no one should pray to any man or god but you, didn't you? Well, Daniel is paying no attention to you or your decree! He still prays three times a day to his God." The king sadly listened to the men's accusations. He realized that he had been tricked, and he began looking for a way to save Daniel. At sundown, Daniel's accusers came back to see the king again, just to remind him that he had to do what he had promised to do in his decree. There was nothing Darius could do: Daniel had to be thrown to the lions!

The king ordered Daniel thrown into the lions' den. The last thing he said to Daniel was, "May your God, whom you serve continually, rescue you." A large stone was placed over the opening to the lions' den, and the king sealed it with his own signet ring and the rings of his nobles so no one could open it and rescue Daniel. Then, the king went to his palace and spent the night without sleeping or eating. He even refused all the entertainment offered to him. He was too concerned about Daniel to think of anything else. As soon as it began to get light outside, the king hurried to the lions' den. He shouted to Daniel, "Has your God been able to rescue you from the lions?" He was thrilled to hear Daniel himself shout out that God had shut the mouths of the lions and kept him safe throughout the night.

Daniel was lifted out of the lions' den and there wasn't a scratch on him! Darius was so angry at the way Daniel's enemies had tricked him, he had them thrown into the lions' den. The lions pounced on the wicked men and killed them before their feet touched the floor of the den. Then King Darius wrote a decree that everyone in his kingdom should fear and honor Daniel's God, "for he rescues and he saves; he performs signs and wonders in the heavens and on the earth."

"Daniel and the Lions" Rap

Directions: Divide students into two groups—Daniel and the lions. Have them read the rap together, keeping the rhythm going by snapping their fingers or clapping their hands.

Daniel:	Some men were jealous of me, you see,
	So they came up with a plot to get rid of me.
	They got Darius to say a foolish thing:
	Everyone had to pray only to the king!
Lions:	Those who disobeyed would be thrown in
	With us lions in our den. Growwwl!
Daniel:	I prayed to God as I did every day.
	When my enemies saw me, they ran to say,
	"Oh, king, we saw Daniel and we know he was
	Praying to his God like he always does.
	He deserves to die because he didn't obey.
	You made the rule and now Daniel must pay!"
Lions:	We watched the king order his men,
	And they threw Daniel into our den.
	We were really hungry, but do you know what?
	We couldn't eat Daniel 'cause our mouths stayed shut!
Daniel:	God was with me and all through the night
	Those lions couldn't take even one small bite.
Lions:	We were hungry all night; didn't eat a thing.
	Then early next morning we heard the king:
	"Daniel, did God save you as you said?"
Daniel:	"I'm fine," I said. "I'm alive, not dead!"

A Description of God

Directions: Solve the clues, then use the words to complete what King Darius said about Daniel's God. The first letter of some of the clues are given to help you. Look up Daniel 6:26–27 to check your work.

CLUES

1. Another word for saved r___ ___ ___ ___ ___ ___ ___
2. Always, without end f___ ___ ___ ___ ___ ___ ___
3. Another word for miracles w___ ___ ___ ___ ___ ___ ___
4. Opposite of dying ___ ___ ___ ___ ___ ___
5. Ruined, demolished d___ ___ ___ ___ ___ ___ ___ ___ ___
6. Another word for rescues ___ ___ ___ ___ ___
7. This planet we live on ___ ___ ___ ___ ___
8. Might, strength p___ ___ ___ ___ ___

For he is the ___ ___ ___ ___ ___ ___ (4) God and he endures

___ ___ ___ ___ ___ ___ ___ (2); his kingdom will not be

___ ___ ___ ___ ___ ___ ___ ___ ___ (5), his dominion will never end.

He rescues and he ___ ___ ___ ___ ___ (6); he performs signs and

___ ___ ___ ___ ___ ___ ___ (3) in the heavens and on the

___ ___ ___ ___ ___ (7). He has ___ ___ ___ ___ ___ ___ ___ (1)

Daniel from the ___ ___ ___ ___ ___ (8) of the lions.

©Teacher Created Resources, Inc.

Picture Puzzle

Directions: Color the pieces of the puzzle. Then, cut them out and try to fit them together to make a picture of the Bible story found in Daniel 6.

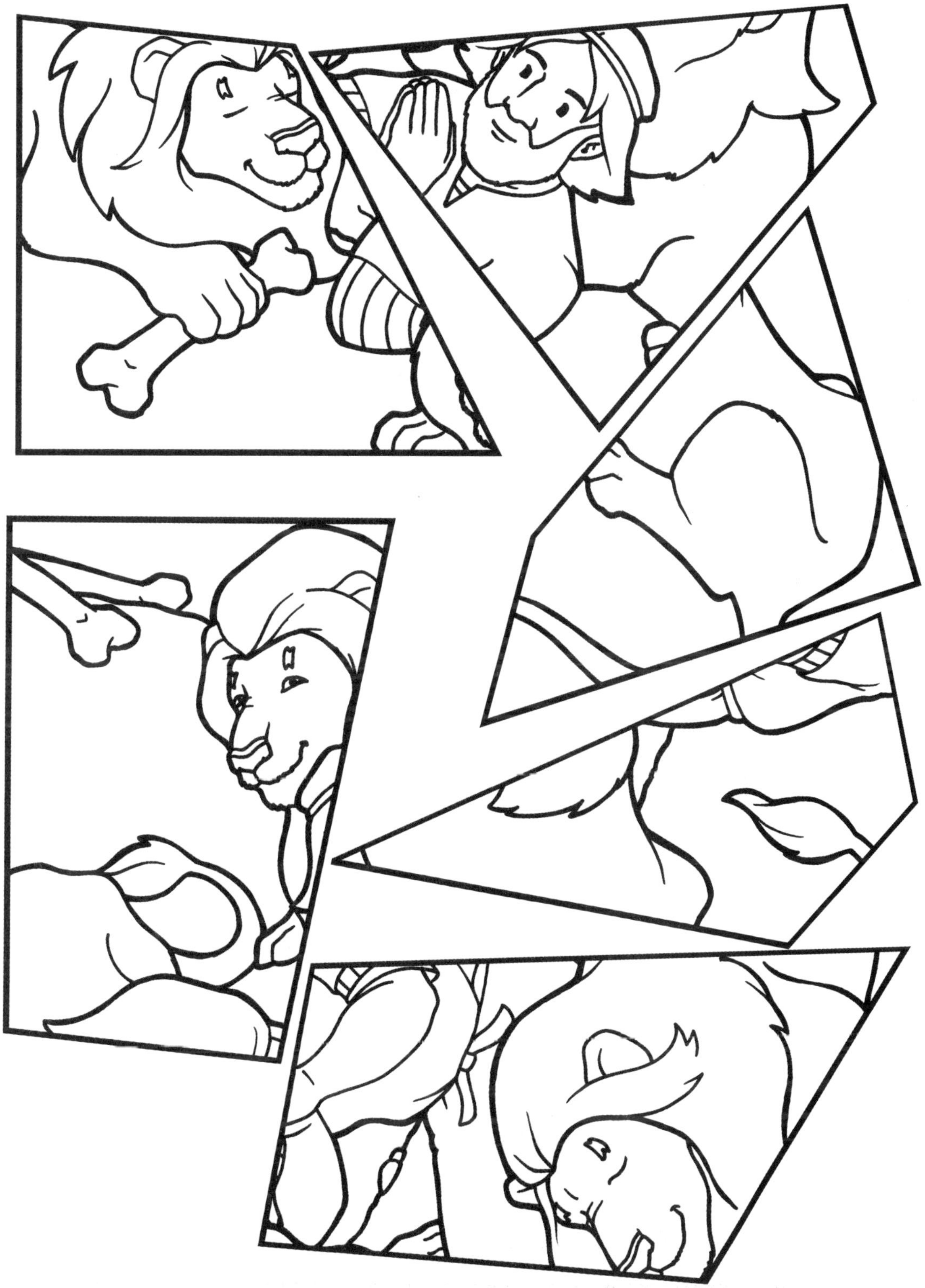

Why Be Like Daniel?

Directions: Daniel is a good example for all of us to follow. Why? Follow the directions to find out. Look up Daniel 6:4b to check your work.

- Cross out all six-letter words
- Cross out all words that rhyme with *cook*.
- Cross out all words that begin with **G**.
- Cross out all words that end with **H**.
- Write the remaining words in order on the lines below the box.

BODIES	THEY	GOD	COULD	TOOK
FIND	WATCH	SHOOK	NO	GONE
FOLLOW	CORRUPTION	IN	GROW	WASH
HIM	FATHER	BECAUSE	BOOK	WISHES
HE	WAS	FAITH	GLORY	BOTH
TRUSTWORTHY	AND	LOOK	NEITHER	GRACE
ANIMAL	CORRUPT	NOR	TEACH	HOOK
GREAT	GOOD	NEGLIGENT	MOTHER	WITH

"__________ __________ __________ __________

__________ __________ __________,

__________ __________ __________

__________ __________ __________

__________ __________ __________."

If you don't know what all those words mean, look them up in a dictionary to find out.

 ©Teacher Created Resources, Inc.

Dot-to-Dot Picture

Directions: Daniel did not let the king's decree stop him from praying. Connect the numbered dots to find out where he prayed. Look up Daniel 6:10 to see if you are right.

Prayer Wheel

Like Daniel, you have many reasons to pray every day. Make this prayer wheel to remind you of when to pray.

Materials

- patterns on pages 44 and 45
- cardstock
- crayons or colored markers
- scissors
- brad fastener

Directions

1. Copy the circles on this page and page 45 onto cardstock.
2. Color and cut out the circles.
3. Poke a hole in the center of each circle.
4. Insert a brad fastener to connect the circles together. The circle with the cut-out window should go on top.
5. Turn the bottom circle to the reason for praying and read the Bible verse.

Prayer Wheel Pattern

Prayer Wheel

Prayer Wheel Pattern

See page 44 for directions.

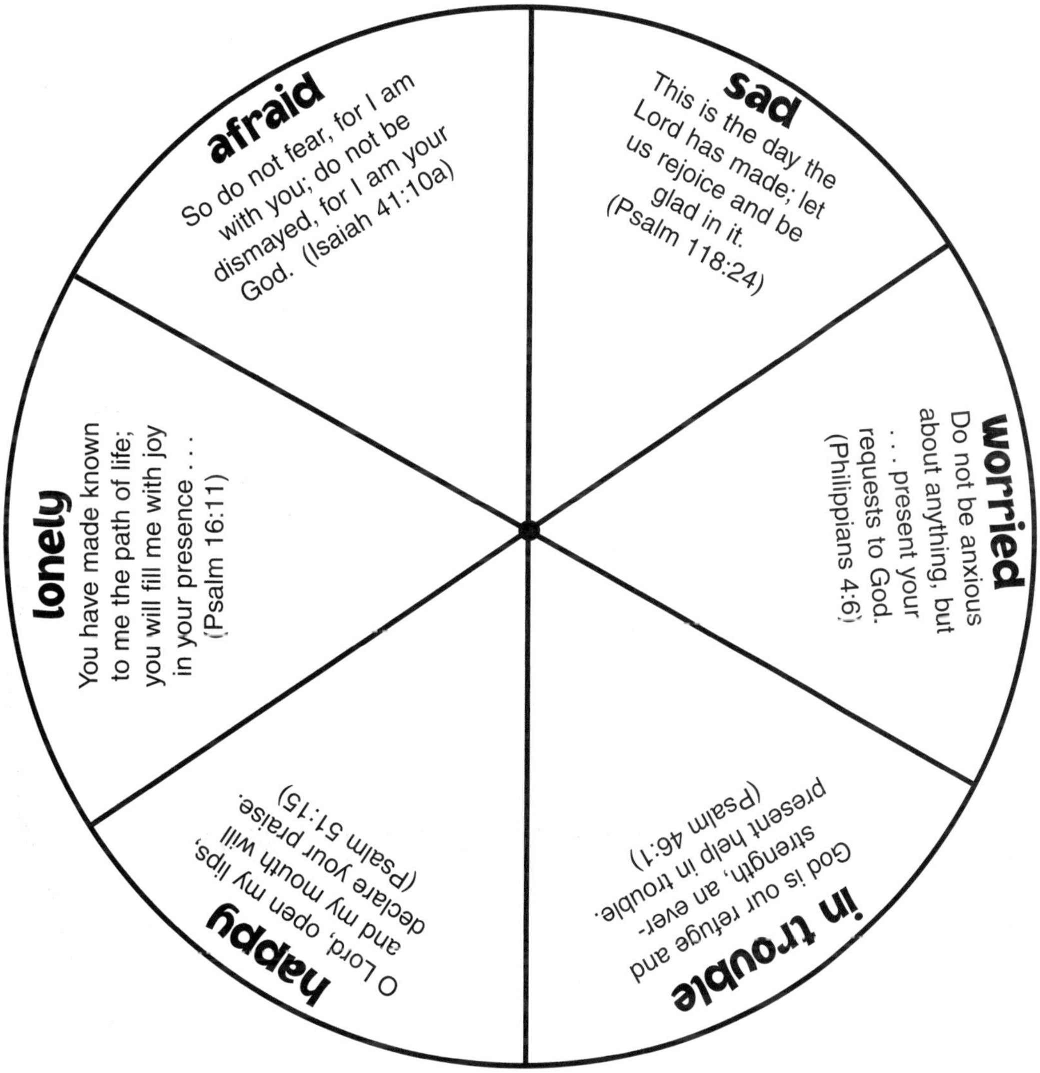

Daniel's Faith Song

Directions: Sing the song below.

(**Tune:** "Row, Row, Row Your Boat")

Daniel prayed to God every single day.
Everybody in the land knew this was Daniel's way.

Then the king was tricked to make a grand decree
That said "No one can pray at all to anyone but me!"

Daniel didn't stop what he did each day.
Three times a day he prayed to God 'cause that was Daniel's way.

Daniel's enemies reported what they saw.
They told the king to punish him because he broke the law.

Darius tried very hard to protect his friend,
But at last he had to throw him in the lions' den!

Daniel wasn't scared; he trusted God that night.
And God shut the lions' mouths so they couldn't bite.

Then King Darius made a new law right away,
That everyone should honor God and worship Him each day!

Answer Key

Page 7

TO THESE FOUR YOUNG MEN GOD GAVE KNOWLEDGE AND UNDERSTANDING OF ALL KINDS OF LITERATURE AND LEARNING. AND DANIEL COULD UNDERSTAND VISIONS AND DREAMS OF ALL KINDS.

Page 9

11. KI **N** G'S
2. J **E** RUSALEM
1. **B** ABYLON
4. YO **U** NG
3. **C** HIEF OF COURT OFFICIALS
5. **H** ANDSOME
7. H **A** NANIAH
8. **D** ANIEL
12. WI **N** E
6. W **E** LL INFORMED
Z
9. A **Z** ARIAH
10. MISH **A** EL
13. TH **R** EE YEARS

Page 13

The following foods are circled: corn, carrots, onions, beans, and tomatoes.

Empty box should have water drawn in it.

Page 15

HE CHANGES TIMES AND SEASONS; HE SETS UP KINGS AND DEPOSES THEM. HE GIVES WISDOM TO THE WISE AND KNOWLEDGE TO THE DISCERNING . . . . HE KNOWS WHAT LIES IN DARKNESS, AND LIGHT DWELLS WITH HIM. (Daniel 2:21–22)

Page 17

1. B, C, G, J
2. E, K
3. A, D, F, H, I, K
4. D, I, K

Page 18

K	Z	R	M	Y	S	T	E	R	Y	L	T	E	L	L
N	D	R	E	A	M	R	Q	C	U	G	G	L	D	C
O	D	D	H	V	O	Z	A	W	B	L	T	Y	Z	A
W	W	G	V	N	E	J	V	N	D	R	E	A	M	N
N	I	J	O	Q	T	A	Z	F	S	N	N	R	B	N
H	S	H	B	D	V	W	L	P	R	W	Q	L	Q	O
K	E	S	U	B	M	I	T	S	Z	L	E	M	N	T
M	R	E	X	P	L	A	I	N	C	H	A	R	G	E

JOSEPH: dream, dream, cannot, God, answer, known, wise, charge, submit

DANIEL: tell, explain, mystery, reveals, honor, high, ruler

Page 19

2	1
4	6
3	5

Page 23

1. NATIONS
2. KINGDOM
3. ETERNAL
4. WONDERS
5. WORLD
6. SIGNS
7. PLEASURE

KING NEBUCHADNEZZAR, TO THE PEOPLES, NATIONS AND MEN OF EVERY LANGUAGE, WHO LIVE IN ALL THE WORLD: . . . IT IS MY PLEASURE TO TELL YOU ABOUT THE MIRACULOUS SIGNS AND WONDERS THAT THE MOST HIGH GOD HAS PERFORMED FOR ME. HOW GREAT ARE HIS SIGNS, HOW MIGHTY HIS WONDERS! HIS KINGDOM IS AN ETERNAL KINGDOM; HIS DOMINION ENDURES FROM GENERATION TO GENERATION.

Page 24

Renounce your sins by doing what is right, and your wickedness by being kind to the oppressed.

Answer Key

Page 25

THIS IS LOVE FOR GOD:
TO OBEY HIS COMMANDS.

Page 26

PRIDE GOES BEFORE DESTRUCTION, A HAUGHTY SPIRIT BEFORE A FALL.

Page 31

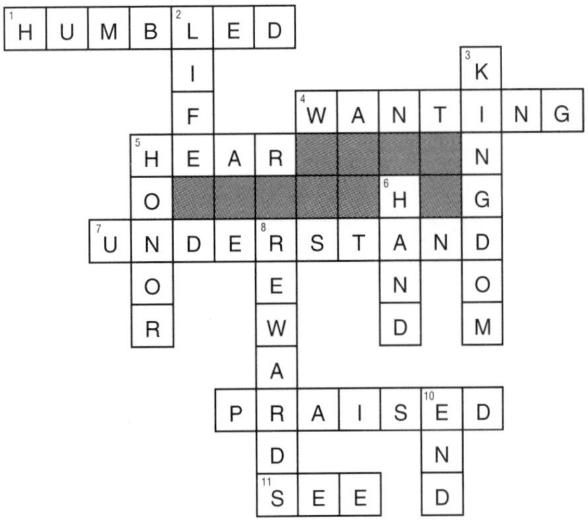

Page 32

1. God
2. divided
3. weighed
4. days
5. end
6. scales
7. you
8. kingdom

Page 33

Page 34

6	2
4	1
5	3

Page 36

Daniel: A, D, E

Belshazzar: B, C, F

Page 40

1. rescued
2. forever
3. wonders
4. living
5. destroyed
6. saves
7. earth
8. power

Page 41

Page 42

THEY COULD FIND NO CORRUPTION IN HIM, BECAUSE HE WAS TRUSTWORTHY AND NEITHER CORRUPT NOR NEGLIGENT.

Page 43

 ©Teacher Created Resources, Inc.